THE CHANGING FACE OF
GREECE

Text by TAMSIN OSLER
Photography by CHRIS FAIRCLOUGH

Published by Raintree, a division of Reed Elsevier, Inc.

Library of Congress Cataloging-in-Publication Data

Cataloging-in-publication data is available at the Library of Congress

ISBN 0-7398-6039-9

Printed in Hong Kong
1234567890
LB 07 06 05 04 03

Acknowledgments
The publishers would like to thank the following for their contributions to this book: Rob Bowden—statistics research; Peter Bull—map illustration; Nick Hawken—statistics panel illustrations. All photographs are by Chris Fairclough except: WTPix (Alan Towse) 18; Eye Ubiquitous 20; Travel Ink 27.

Contents

1 Yánnina: A Changing Town

Yánnina is the capital of the Epirus region of north-western Greece. It lies on the shores of Lake Pamvótis surrounded by the high mountains of the Pindus range. Because of its location, Yánnina and other nearby towns and villages were quite isolated until after the 1960s. In the 1950s and 1960s thousands of people left Yánnina and migrated abroad or to the capital, Athens. Since then, however, there have been great improvements in the region's road network, and Yánnina is now well-connected with Athens and other Greek cities.

Although agriculture has steadily declined in the region, the city is still famous for its yogurt, cheese, and other dairy products, while intensive poultry-rearing has become an important new industry in the nearby countryside. Yánnina is also well known for its tradition of metalworking and jewelry making. Greek and foreign tourists visit Yánnina to see its rich cultural history and, nearby, some of the most spectacular scenery in Greece.

Yánnina has one of Greece's largest universities, which has greatly increased the number of young people living in the city. Since 1971 the city's population has increased by more than a third. It is continuing to grow as more housing, new public buildings, hotels, and other facilities are constructed. Although since the 1950s Yánnina has lost much of its traditional architecture, it still preserves a bustling old quarter with narrow streets and stone houses with wooden balconies. Yánnina, an example of the changing face of Greece, has transformed from a remote market town into a modern and vibrant city with a fascinating mix of old and new, of traditional and modern.

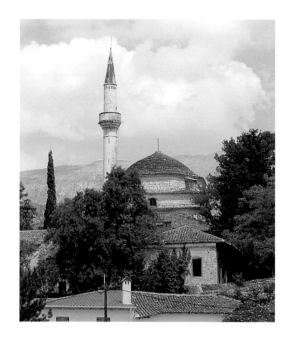

▲ *The Aslan Pasha Mosque within Yánnina's ancient fortress was built by Aslan Pasha in 1618.*

▼ *This modern luxury hotel, near Lake Pamvótis, is built in the architectural style of a traditional local mansion.*

▲ This map shows the main geographical features of Greece, as well as places mentioned in this book.

GREECE: KEY FACTS

Area: 50,949 square miles (131,957 square kilometers)
Population: 10,939,771 (2001 census)
Population density: 215.4 people per square mile (83.2 people per square kilometer)
Capital city: Athens
Other main cities: Thessaloníki (Salonika), Piraeus, Patras
Highest mountain: Mount Olympus 9,570 feet (2,917 meters)
Longest river: Aliakmon 185 miles (297 kilometers)
Main language: Modern Greek
Main religions: Greek Orthodoxy (98 percent), Muslim (1.5 percent)
Currency: Euro

Past Times

The Heritage of Ancient Greece

The history of Greece spans 4,000 years. Ancient Greek culture and civilization, which flourished around the shores of the Mediterranean, reached its peak around 500 B.C.E., producing some of the world's greatest artists, dramatists, politicians, philosophers, mathematicians, doctors, and scientists. In the second century B.C.E., Greece fell to the Romans. When, in 330 C.E., the Roman Empire was split in two, the eastern Greek-speaking part formed the Byzantine Empire. Afer 1,000 C.E., a succession of foreign peoples invaded Greece, and by the late 1500s it had been absorbed into the Ottoman Empire.

The Beginnings of Modern Greece

Greece was dominated by Ottoman Turkish rule for nearly 400 years. In 1821 the Greeks rebelled against their Turkish rulers, winning their independence in 1830. However, Greece was much smaller than it is today, since much of the country did not gain independence until the late 1800s and during the Balkan Wars of 1912–1913.

▲ The Acropolis, built in the 5th century B.C.E, presides over the skyline of modern Athens.

◄ The Greek Parliament building overlooks Syntagma Square. In the foreground are members of the National Guard, the Évzones, in Greek national dress.

During World War II, Greece was occupied by Germany. Following its liberation in 1945, the country was plunged almost immediately into a civil war (1946–1949) in which the Communist Left was defeated. Greece was thus in alignment with the West. In 1952 Greece joined NATO (North Atlantic Treaty Organization).

New Government

In 1967 a group of military colonels overthrew the government. Their military dictatorship lasted until 1974, when a student revolution helped cause its downfall. Since then Greece has been a parliamentary democracy with an elected parliament led by a president. In 1981 Greece joined the European Union (EU). In 2002, the Euro (the currency of the EU) replaced the Greek drachma, the oldest currency in the world.

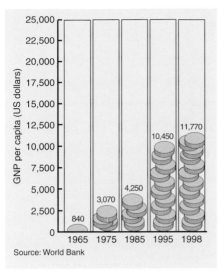

▲ *The revenue Greece earns from goods and services it produces has increased dramatically since 1965.*

IN THEIR OWN WORDS

My name is Élena Nazíri. I live in Trikala in the plain of Thessaly. Trikala was in Turkish hands for hundreds of years. Nazir isn't a Greek name; it's Turkish. My great-grandfather took a Turkish name, but he also fought in the resistance against the Turks. This part of Greece wasn't liberated until 1881.

Life for people today is changing so rapidly. When my father was growing up, they had no electricity at home. He had a good education, though. Now people have air conditioning in their homes and lots of other luxuries. Everyone has cars. It's easy to travel from one place to another. Greece is like one big village now.

Landscape and Climate

Greece is Europe's southernmost country. Situated at the end of the Balkan landmass, mainland Greece forms a peninsula jutting out into the Mediterranean Sea. Greece is also an archipelago of some two thousand islands, although only 170 of them are inhabited. It is a country of varied landscape and climate. Tourist postcards usually depict its sandy beaches, blue seas, and hot sunshine, but in fact three-quarters of Greece is mountainous country, and its winters can be very cold and wet.

Mountains

The Pindus Mountains, running from north to south, form the backbone of mainland Greece. In the northeast, creating the border with Bulgaria, are the Rhodope Mountains. Other mountains include the Taygetus in the Peloponnese (a peninsula) and the White Mountains of Crete.

Greece's mountains form many steep cliffs and deep, narrow gorges with rivers running through them. Their slopes may be forested with beech, oak, chestnut, and pine, or covered with dense, thorny scrub. Elsewhere, as in the Mani region of the Peloponnese, the limestone slopes are dry, rocky, and barren, resembling stony deserts.

▲ *Land rising up steeply from the sea is typical of much of the Greek coastline.*

▼ *In early May the lower slopes of this hillside village provide rich pasture land, while the peaks above often still have snow.*

IN THEIR OWN WORDS

My name is Grigoris Kitsoulis. I'm 82 years old. I have lived all my life in this village, Polystafyllo, in the Epirus. When I was young I used to go hunting in the woods for rabbits and birds. These were luxury foods for our family. Many people around here used to hunt. They hunted wild boar, wolves, foxes, and rabbits. There aren't many animals in the woods today. In twenty years, this will be an abandoned place. The houses will only be used as vacation homes. Nobody will take care of the landscape and the wilderness will return.

The climate is changing, too. We used to have much more snow. It doesn't seem to snow so often here, and it rains a lot less, too. It often used to rain for ten to twenty days at a time. That's rare today.

Lowlands

Most of Greece's lowlands stretch along its coastal areas. The three main inland lowlands are the plains of Thessaly in central Greece, Macedonia in the north, and Thrace in the northeast. Fertile lowlands are also found in the Peloponnese.

Islands

The landscape of the Greek islands varies greatly. The Ionian Islands off the west coast of Greece are green and comparatively lush due to heavy winter rainfall. In contrast, the Cyclades islands in the Aegean Sea are rocky, dry, and wind-swept. Crete, which separates the Aegean from the rest of the Mediterranean Sea, has high arid peaks with lower green slopes and fertile plains.

▼ *In the foreground of this view across the Gulf of Corinth to mainland Greece are olive trees and tall, dark cypresses, which are typical of the Greek landscape.*

Climate

The summers in Greece are generally hot and dry, and the winters mild and wet. However, temperature and rainfall patterns vary considerably between northern and southern Greece and between coastal and mountain regions. In winter, the average January temperature in the northern city of Thessaloníki is around 42.8°F (6°C), although it can drop as low as 24.8°F (-4°C).

In Heráklion, on the southern island of Crete, January temperatures average 52°F (11°C). Summer temperatures tend to vary less, averaging 82.4°F (28°C) in July but often reaching highs of 104°F (40°C). In northern and mountainous regions, the winter often brings heavy snowfalls, and during the winter Crete's high peaks may have snow on them, while the sea below is warm enough for swimming.

▲ *Farmers irrigating their crops in the plains of central Greece*

Forest Fires

Greece's hot, dry summer months bring the threat of forest fires. Following devastating fires in 1998, the number of firefighters, fire stations, and fire-fighting equipment available in high-risk areas was greatly increased. The authorities run seminars for people living near forests that explain how to combat the danger of fire. Every summer, posters, billboards, and announcements on television warn against the risk of fires. Since the late 1990s, the loss of land to fire has dropped dramatically.

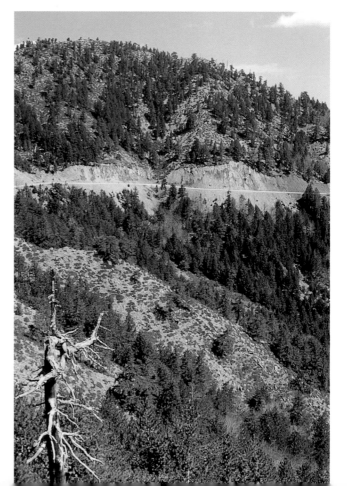

▶ *A mountain pass winds through conifer woods in central Greece.*

Earthquakes

Greece lies on more than one fault line in the earth's crust, and mild tremors are not uncommon. One fault line runs from north to south along the west coast of Greece and down to the Peloponnese. In 1986 Kalamata and some surrounding villages were devastated by an earthquake that left more than 12,000 people homeless. Many poorly constructed buildings from the 1960s were destroyed. In 1999 Athens was hit by an earthquake that made thousands homeless, but that fortunately caused few deaths. The Greek Army is trained to act swiftly to provide emergency shelter, water, and relief supplies.

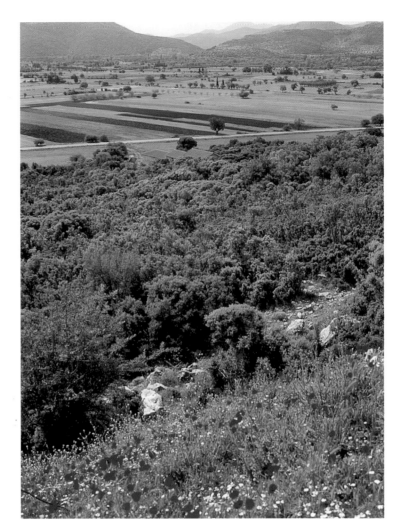

▶ *Looking at this peaceful scene, it is hard to imagine that parts of Greece lie on fault lines and have experienced damaging earthquakes.*

IN THEIR OWN WORDS

I'm Grigoris Mihos. I'm 13 years old and I live in a village near the town of Préveza, on the west coast of Greece. There are very high mountains all around us. Look, even now in May, you can see snow on them. Our water comes from the mountains. It rains a lot here so we rarely have problems with water shortages, but I know it's a problem for many villages, especially if there are factories or industries in the area that use a lot of water. We're lucky. In summer it gets very hot here, and the mosquitoes are a big problem, especially around the marshy lands a little further south.

Energy Sources

Most of Greece's electricity is generated by power stations fueled by lignite (poor quality brown coal), which is mined from the Pindus Mountains. Greece's energy needs have been increasing steadily, and burning lignite, although cheap, causes pollution. As a result, the government has banned the construction of new lignite power stations and hopes instead to increase the number of plants burning natural gas. Approximately 10 percent of Greece's energy is generated by hydroelectricity.

Greece has vast renewable energy sources in the form of sunlight, wind, and wave power, but there has been slow progress in developing these resources. Solar panels on rooftops are widely used to heat hot water, but solar power plants are extremely expensive to build and, to date, none have been built. There are wind farms on Crete, Naxos, and other Aegean islands, and the next decade is likely to see the construction of many more.

▲ Solar panels and television aerials sit on the roof of a typical modern Greek house.

◄ This modern oil refinery is on the outskirts of Corinth, in the northeast section of the Peloponnese.

Agriculture

Although less than 30 percent of Greece is farmable land, historically the Greek economy was based on agriculture. Rural people lived by subsistence farming, relying on their flocks of sheep and goats for milk, cheese, yogurt, and meat, and on their vineyards and olive trees for wine and olive oil. In the last few decades, subsistence farming has declined rapidly. However, farmers have increased their agricultural output as subsidies from the EU have helped to modernize their farming practices. Greece's principal products are olive oil, olives, citrus fruit, corn, wheat, cotton, rice, and grapes. In recent decades the factory-farming of pigs and chickens has increased. In the case of tobacco, however, the EU has subsidized a decrease in its production to reduce cigarette consumption, which grew by 6 percent in the 1990s.

▲ *Market gardeners use plastic tunnels to extend the growing season of vegetables and other crops.*

IN THEIR OWN WORDS

My full name is Evángelos Grigoríou, but Evángelos is commonly shortened to Lakis. I'm a farmer. Agriculture is not an easy way of life in a country as rocky as this. Fortunately, we get plenty of rain here. We used to have many more animals, including cows, horses, and donkeys. You don't see a lot of cows in Greece because they need better pasture land than sheep and goats do. We still have goats, so we have our own milk from which to make cheese and yogurt.

Until the 1950s there were few tractors around here. People used donkeys to transport their crops and firewood. They rode their donkeys, too. Since the 1970s all the local farmers use tractors. They've made their fields bigger, too. If I were twenty years old now, I'd choose to go to school first and then come back here to farm as a better farmer.

Fishing

Greeks have lived off fish from their seas for thousands of years. In the past the population of many Greek islands depended almost exclusively on fishing for a living. Greek fish markets usually display a wide diversity of fish, ranging from small fish such as whitebait and sardines to large fish such as swordfish, grouper, and tuna. Local seafood also includes lobster, sea urchin, octopus, cuttlefish, squid, and mussel. However, overfishing and water pollution have reduced fish stocks. The government is trying to improve the situation by regulating the number of commercial fishing licences and introducing fishing quotas. Restrictions have also been introduced on certain fishing methods, and against catching fish that are too small and young to breed. Meanwhile local supply cannot satisfy demand, especially during the tourist season. As a result, Greece now imports a wide range of fresh and frozen fish from Israel and East Asia and mackerel and cod from the North Sea. With the exception of farmed fish (see page 41), exports tend to be limited to large tuna, which is exported to Japan and other parts of Asia.

▲ *A colorful array of native fish (sea bream, sea bass, and octopus) and imported salmon in a fish market*

▼ *Greeks often buy fresh seafood directly from fishermen at the harborside.*

IN THEIR OWN WORDS

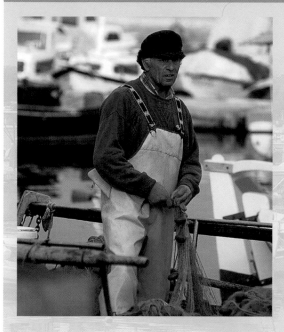

My name is Dimítris Páppas. I have been going fishing since my uncle used to take me as a small boy. His boat didn't have an engine like most boats have now. In the evening we would row out to sea to drop the nets. Then we would go out again in the very early hours to collect them. Fish has always been a staple part of the modern Greek diet just as it was for the ancient Greeks. Greater awareness of the benefits of eating more fish, and recent scares about possible diseases associated with meat, have made a lot of people want to eat more fish. But things are getting harder because there are far fewer fish out there. I sell my catch locally—to the restaurants around here, and in the town market.

Minerals

Greece is rich in a variety of minerals. It has large reserves of bauxite, which is used to make aluminium, and it produces some 36 percent of the EU's natural magnesite (used in medicine, fertilizers, and in industry). Greece also mines zinc (used with copper to make brass, and to galvanize steel), iron ore (for iron and steel), and lead. Marble has been quarried in Greece since ancient times and is still widely used today. The manufacturing of cement, which is produced from limestone, is a primary industry. Greece is second to China in world production of cement.

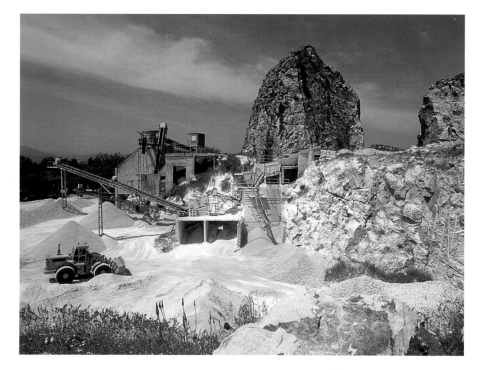

▲ *Limestone quarries such as this one are found all over Greece.*

5

The Changing Environment

Urbanization

In the last fifty years Greece has experienced urbanization on a huge scale. After World War II, industrial growth around Athens caused the population to soar, as people came to the city looking for work and a better life. This has transformed Athens from a city of about 700,000 into an urban sprawl of nearly four million people.

The very swift pace in the growth of Athens resulted in poor city planning. Most people live in apartments in concrete buildings that have balconies but no yards. Below, the streets are noisy, congested, and full of traffic. The shortages in housing are a huge problem. The city has very few green or open spaces. Meanwhile, new buildings are continuously encroaching on the rural areas around Athens and Piraeus. However, most people who work in Athens want to live within the city, since its transportation system and roads do not allow for a quick and easy commute to work.

Sources: 1950, 1970 and 2000 from Geographical Digest; 2015 from United Nations Development Programme

▲ *The number of people living in urban areas has increased dramatically in the last fifty years.*

◄ *Athens contains both ancient archaeological sites and lots of new building work.*

Athens and Air Pollution

Athens lies in a plain surrounded by hills on three sides. This contributes greatly to its pollution problems, since traffic fumes and industrial smog are trapped above the city. During very hot weather, the city's pollution can cause health and respiratory problems, especially among the elderly and the sick. Acid rain has also caused damage to the stonework of the city's ancient monuments.

The city's authorities now monitor pollution levels in order to predict and prevent pollution crises. To reduce traffic, drivers are only allowed to use their cars on certain days and traffic is diverted away from congested areas. Cars are not allowed at all in many inner-city areas. More recently, there has been huge investment in Athens' public transportation system.

▲ *Athens's yellow trolleys complement the city's extensive network of buses.*

IN THEIR OWN WORDS

My name is Maria Kóllia. I come from the north of Greece, from a mountain village near Kozáni, in Macedonia. I am a teacher of English in a foreign-language school. I came to live in Athens because of the better work prospects here. But Athens is not an easy place to live, and it continues to get harder. The city is overcrowded. Athens' biggest problem is the traffic. People's health is suffering.

I think the government is not doing enough to help the overpopulation problem of Greece's cities. I fear that they will continue to grow. Public money should be distributed more evenly throughout the different regions of the country. This would help limit migration toward the cities. Fortunately, village life has become much better due to improvements in living conditions, as well as in transportation and communication. Some young people now are choosing to remain in the country. I will return there when I retire.

Water Pollution

As in other places in the Mediterranean Sea, pollution is a problem in Greek waters. In the early days following Greece's industrialization, the sea around urban centers served as a dumping ground for sewage and industrial waste. Increases in the use of fertilizers and pesticides in farming also contributed to river and sea water pollution.

However, great improvements have been made in waste management and reduction in the use of harmful chemicals near sources of drinking water. Today, over 90 percent of Greece's coastal waters are fit for bathing.

▲ *Water pollution is a problem in Greece. In recent years this situation has greatly improved.*

Water Shortages

Water shortages have always been a problem in Greece, especially in areas that have to rely on water being brought in by shipping tankers. Households commonly use cisterns or underground tanks to store rainwater, which is collected from the roofs. Tourism, farming and agriculture are placing a huge pressure on Greece's water supplies.

Many Greek farmers pump water up from wells that draw from the underground water

▶*In mountainous areas river beds can rapidly fill with water during times of heavy rainfall.*

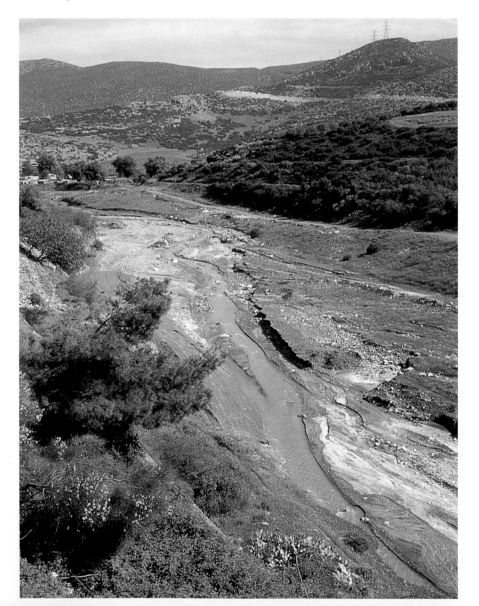

IN THEIR OWN WORDS

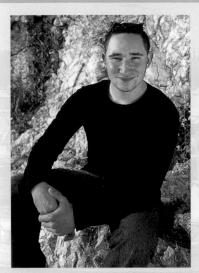

I am Níkos Agelídis. I am 16 years old and live with my family in Athens. It's a very noisy city. As well as all the cars, taxis, and buses, lots of people use motor scooters and motorcycles to weave in and out of the traffic. The motorcycles are very noisy. It's hardly ever quiet in the center of Athens. The authorities should do a lot more to limit noise levels.

In school we are taught about the environment for about one hour every week. Even so, we are not as aware of the environment as I think we should be. It's not good to see garbage lying around in the city. Police should be given more power to fine people who drop litter and who make unnecessary noise.

table. The government is trying to persuade farmers to grow crops that do not need heavy irrigation. Meanwhile, households and businesses that have high water-consumption levels have had to deal with water rationing and increased water prices.

Noise Pollution

In many of Greece's major cities, the number of people living in a relatively small area has created problems with noise pollution. The combined effect of car horns, motor scooters, traffic, and air-conditioning units creates a level of noise that can be stressful to live near. The long working day and a tradition of socializing until late into the night mean that there are very few hours of calm. The quietest hours of the day are during the midafternoon siesta, when many shops close and people return home for an afternoon rest.

▶ *Because of pedestrian and traffic congestion in Athens, it is seldom quiet in the city.*

Tourism

Greece is one of the world's most popular vacation destinations, with more than twelve million foreign visitors each year. Inevitably this has had an enormous impact on Greece's landscape and environment. It has also placed great pressures on the country's infrastructure, including its water supplies, waste disposal, road building, and agriculture. Huge areas of Greece's island coastlines have been developed to appeal to tourists, with hotels, swimming pools, restaurants, and bars. On some islands, many local people have given up their self-sufficient way of life, and even their land, in favor of building and owning a hotel, bar, or souvenir shop. Olive groves and vineyards are no longer tended, since people buy produce rather than grow their own. Traditional stone houses have been abandoned or torn down to build new concrete houses and apartment buildings. A disregard for building regulations means that there has been very little control of how and where construction has taken place. However, the authorities are increasingly taking steps to control new development.

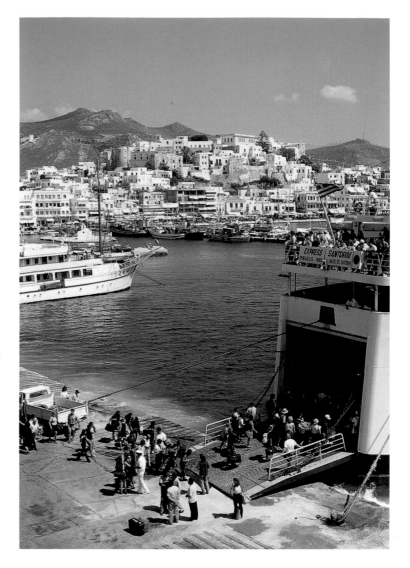

▲ Ferries take tourists from the mainland to the many beautiful Greek islands.

◀ The tunnels under the Pindus Mountains will form part of the Egnatía Odós, a major highway that will link the international port of Igoumenitsa with the central and eastern side of Greece.

In recent years the Greek tourist industry has been looking at ways to appeal to wealthy visitors who are willing to spend money on expensive accomodations and facilities. Nationally, the Greek government is supporting the construction of more harbors and yacht marinas to promote Greece as a cruising and sailing destination. Locally, a growing number of tourist enterprises are promoting ecotourism and special-interest vacations centered around, for example, bird watching in northern Greece, mountain trekking in the Epirus, or wildflower spotting in Crete. Such developments mean the spread of tourism to areas of Greece other than its coast and archaeological sites, as well as a longer tourist season.

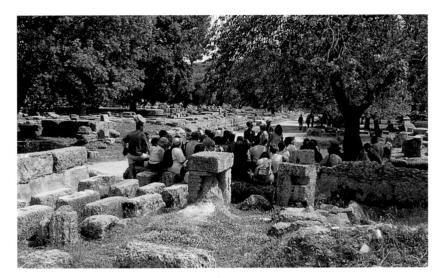

▲ *A group of tourists at the ancient site of Olympia*

IN THEIR OWN WORDS

My name is Voúla Theodoráki. I work as a tour guide here on the island of Póros, off the coast of the Peloponnese. Tourism on the island really took off in the 1970s, and by the early 1980s it was booming. Ninety percent of the island's economy is dependent on it. The increase in tourism does put the island under pressure, though. Sometimes, in the height of the tourist season when the island is full, the local water supply doesn't meet the demand. Water has to be brought from the mainland. Occasionally we have problems with the power supply, too. Litter can be a problem. Fortunately we have many more garbage cans than we used to, as well as more street sweepers and garbage trucks.

Wildlife Conservation

Greeks have always been passionate about hunting, pursuing animals ranging from wild boar to the smallest birds. The country's once rich wildlife has been greatly depleted, although the mountains are still home to wild boar, bears, wolves, and wildcats, as well as some rare raptors. Today Greece has a substantial number of national parks. As is often the case, however, conservation initiatives are not always welcomed by everyone. For instance, some Greek fishermen used to hunt Mediterranean monk seal—because they saw them as a threat to local fish stocks. A marine reserve in the northern Sporades now protects this endangered seal. On Zante, tourists are urged to keep away from the sandy beaches where the loggerhead sea turtle comes ashore to nest, but some locals see such moves as harmful to their tourist businesses.

Greece has a diversity of wetlands, including river deltas, salt marshes, and lagoons. These areas are remarkably rich in flora and fauna and provide nesting and breeding grounds for water birds including ducks, herons, and a rare species of pelican. A number of bird sanctuaries have been set up in an effort to preserve their populations.

▲ *Tortoises are a common sight in the wild.*

◄ *A sign promoting awareness of the importance of trees and the environment*

A Greener Future?

Greece has lagged far behind most of Europe in confronting its environmental problems. However, public awareness of "green" issues is growing as more and more people take an interest in the state of the environment. Helped by EU funding, the government has put substantial investment into promoting more environmentally sound practices as it improves the country's services and infrastructure. Meanwhile, tourism interests have begun to add urgency to the conservation movement and the protection of places of outstanding natural beauty or of particular historical and architectural interest.

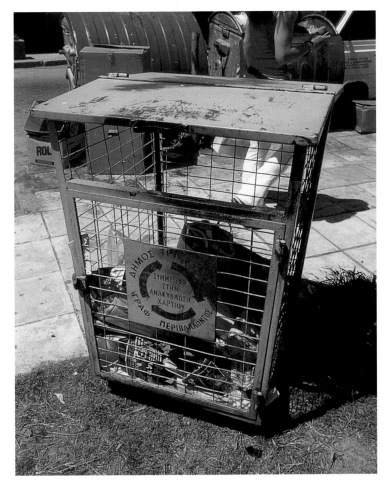

▶ *In provincial towns, recycling facilities are often limited to paper.*

IN THEIR OWN WORDS

My name is Katerína Míta. This is my friend Anna Geládi. I am 15 and she's 13. We live in a residential neighborhood of Athens. Litter isn't a serious problem around here, but it is in other parts of the city. I think people don't think about recycling their garbage because there are very few recycling facilities, limited to certain areas. There is a local tax to cover such services, but I think the government doesn't do enough to provide facilities. There is so much more garbage now than there was in the past. A lot of it has to do with all the packaging used for food.

6

The Changing Population

Population Growth

In the 1950s and 1960s, 10 percent of Greece's population emigrated. The annual birth rate then was about twenty per one thousand people. Today it stands at less than ten per one thousand. Despite these factors, Greece's population has grown from about eight million in the 1950s to nearly eleven million today. The population growth is largely due to a massive influx of migrants, primarily from neighboring Albania, but also from Eastern Europe, the Middle East, and Asia. Today Greece's immigrant population is close to 10 percent of the population, making up a high percentage of the country's unskilled labor force.

▲ *A busy street in central Athens*

Population Distribution

As recently as the 1960s, well over half of Greece's population lived in rural areas. Today over 66 percent live in urban areas, with 40 percent in Athens alone. A further 15 percent of Greeks live in Thessaloniki. Corfu and Crete are two of the most densely populated islands.

Living Longer

Greece has one of the world's largest populations of the elderly. In the late 1990s, 23 percent of the population was elderly. This is expected to rise to 28 percent by 2020. Greek women typically outlive men by five to six years.

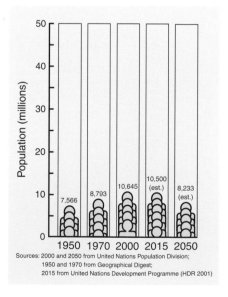

Sources: 2000 and 2050 from United Nations Population Division;
1950 and 1970 from Geographical Digest;
2015 from United Nations Development Programme (HDR 2001)

▲ *This graph shows how population growth in Greece is predicted to decline.*

IN THEIR OWN WORDS

My name is Maria Lavránou. My sister and I grew up in Athens, but both my parents are originally from Corfu. My mother was only 17 when she got married to get away from village life and move to Athens. She had both my sister and me before she was 20. My grandmother came to live with us here so both my parents could go out to work.

My life is very different from my mother's. I am 26 years old now. I am a flautist studying for my master's degree at the Athens Conservatory. I've nearly finished my studies. I'd like to spend the next five years in a steady job, teaching or playing in an orchestra, then settle down to have a family. This is typical of most middle-class families. In the country, people get married a little younger. I still live at home. I don't have enough money to leave home and pay for my schooling. It's quite usual for children to stay with their parents until they're about 28 or even 32. My parents and grandparents ask me from time to time when I'm going to marry, but they aren't pressuring me. They understand that my career is more important. I'd like to have two or three children, but unemployment and the cost of college have to be considered.

Aging parents usually live with one of their children. Care of the elderly typically falls on a daughter or a daughter-in-law. Until recently, Greece had few retirement and nursing homes. This will probably change in the future as the elderly continue to outnumber the young.

▶ *Life expectancy in Greece is one of the highest in the world.*

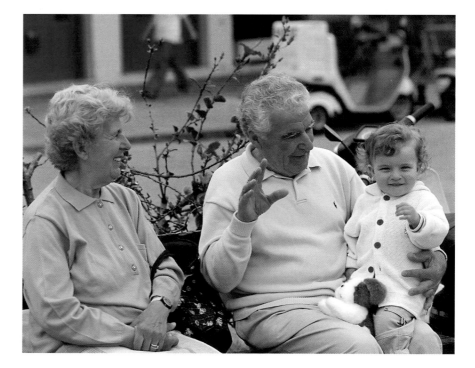

Greece's Minority Populations

Ethnic Greeks form 98 percent of the country's population. The other 2 percent is made up of Turks, Sarakatsans, Vlachs, and Roma, also known as gypsies. Most of Greece's Muslim population is concentrated in Thrace, while the Epirus and Macedonia are home to most Sarakatsans and Vlachs. Traditionally both the Sarakatsans and the Vlachs were nomadic shepherds who moved between the mountains and plains according to where they could find pasture land for their sheep and goats. Unlike the Sarakatsans, who speak a form of Greek, the language of the Vlachs is closer to Latin. Greece's Romany population is concentrated on the mainland, with large numbers now living around Athens's suburbs.

Before World War II, Greece was home to one of the oldest established Jewish communities. Its Jewish population was spread throughout most of Greece's mainland towns, particularly in Thessaloníki and on some of the islands as well. During the German occupation of Greece in World War II, the Greek Jewish community suffered great losses, when thousands were transported to Nazi concentration camps in Eastern Europe. Today there are still Jewish communities in Thessaloníki, Yánnina, and Vólos, with the largest number of Jewish people living in Athens.

▲ Romany women typically dress in brightly colored, patterned clothes and full skirts.

The Greek Diaspora

Greece has a long history of emigration. In the 1950s and 1960s, thousands of people from all parts of the country, many for political as well as economic reasons, went to live and work in Germany, Australia, the United States, or Canada. The large Greek communities they formed in foreign cities are known as the Greek diaspora. Hardly a Greek village exists that has not been affected in some way by emigration. It can be damaging to a community to have so many people leave. However, many communities have also benefited greatly from money made abroad that has been brought or sent back to Greece. Today, apart from large numbers of students going abroad to attend foreign universities, Greece's rate of emigration is low.

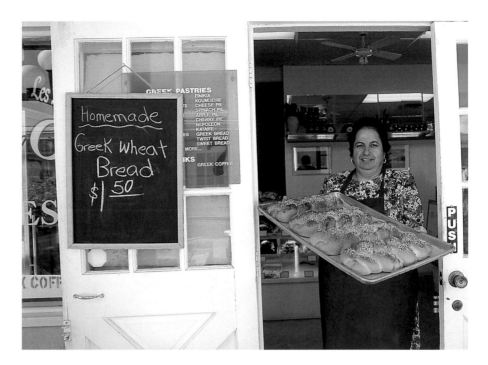

▲ *This Greek woman works in a bakery in Mexico. Her family is one of many that emigrated from Greece.*

IN THEIR OWN WORDS

I am Dashamir Bali. I am Albanian, but I left my home in Tirana, the capital of Albania, in 1993 to come to Greece. I had worked for four years there in the police force. We have great economic problems in our country. I didn't want to leave, but life there was very difficult. I was in my early twenties when I left my mother, father, and brother to come here to find work. I haven't had any problems settling in Greece. At the moment I am working as a waiter. It's hard work, especially at vacation times and during the summer, when the island becomes very busy. I try to go back to Tirana every two months to see my family and my girlfriend. I drive back. It's a long way by car and it takes many hours. I hope that when I have kids, they will be able to have a good life in Albania.

7

Changes at Home

Family Life

Family life is important to most Greeks and exerts a powerful influence on how they live. The traditional Greek household consists of an extended family of several generations living under one roof. This is still true today, although different groups within the extended family may live in separate units in the same apartment building. Family members feel a strong sense of responsibility for each other and depend on one another for emotional, social, and often economic support.

▼ *This extended family gathers to share a meal on Easter Monday. All over Greece, families come together for religious holidays.*

Until recently there was considerable pressure on young people, particularly girls, if, by their late twenties, they had not married or at least become engaged. After marriage, the bride would generally be expected to live with her husband's family. Today couples are choosing to marry later than in the past. They have greater social freedom and may choose to live away from the family home.

In the past, Greek women were expected to provide their husband with a dowry upon marriage. The dowry was usually a combination of money, linen and household goods, farmland, or a building plot. The dowry system was abolished by law in 1983, although it still lingers on, especially in rural areas. Another significant change for Greek women has been that, unlike in the past, they now retain property in their own name after they are married.

The legalization of civil (non religious) marriages in 1982 and the simplification of the divorce process have changed the way marriage is viewed in Greece. In the past, divorce was rare and disapproved of by both the public and the church. In recent years divorce rates have risen dramatically as has the number of single-parent families.

▶ *These young Greeks are likely to marry later than their parents' generation, and they are less likely to stay married.*

IN THEIR OWN WORDS

My name is Angelikí Stávrou. I am 91 years old. I was twenty years old when my husband went to my father to ask for my hand in marriage. I worked on my father's farm then. My husband and I didn't know each other well but we fell in love at a distance. In those days young men and women didn't have many opportunities to mix with each other. When young girls went out, they were usually accompanied by their father or brother. Brothers played a very important role in their sisters' lives. Things are very different today. It would be wonderful to be young now and have the freedom of young people today.

Women's Roles

The lives and experiences of young Greek women today are very different from those of previous generations. Traditionally, Greek girls were brought up to have a domestic role, remaining in the home to look after their husband and family and do the household tasks. If the family had land or animals, they were expected to help with agricultural work, too. Today's young women have the freedom to come and go from their homes, to dress as they like, and to socialize with friends, both male and female. They are encouraged to go to college and to pursue careers and good jobs.

As the Greek way of life has shifted from one based on agriculture to one based on consumerism, it has become increasingly necessary for both parents in a family to go out to work if they wish to maintain a good standard of living. So, although Greek women today have greater independence, life has not necessarily become easier for them as they struggle to cope with the demands of a job, home and family, and a faster and more stressful pace of life.

▲ *Many young Greek women are fashion and fitness conscious.*

◄ *Women on motor scooters are a common sight in Greece's towns and cities.*

Changes in Youth Culture

In recent decades, one of the areas of fastest change has been the interests and pursuits of young people. Greek parents are far less strict with their teenagers than in the past and are more likely to be supportive of their teens' individual interests, talents, and career choices. Children and teenagers today also have many more possessions of their own. Increasing exposure, due mainly to tourism and television, to the fashions, music, and youth culture of Western Europe and the United States means that young Greeks tend to listen to the same music, see the same movies, watch the same or similar television programs, and wear the same fashions as in other Western cultures.

▲ *Most Greek households today have a color television and a VCR.*

IN THEIR OWN WORDS

I'm Victoria Giliánou. I'm 25 and I work in a photographic studio. I enjoy my work, but when I get married and have children, I wouldn't want to work full-time. But part-time work is hard to find in Greece, and it usually is poorly paid. When I get married I will keep my name and add it to my husband's name. This is quite common in Greece. The children don't take their mother's surname, only their father's.

Women are no longer the servants of their husbands as they were in the past. We are educated enough now to have a role equal to that of men. There has to be a balance and now there is. Things will get better for women as they gain a greater say in the work place. I would like to give my daughters a good education. Hopefully, they will speak three foreign languages: English, French, and German or Spanish.

Religion

Nearly all Greeks practice Greek Orthodoxy, a form of
Christianity. There is a small minority of Catholics,
most of whom are found on the Ionian and Aegean islands.
Orthodoxy is central to most Greeks' sense of identity.
Nevertheless, the last 30 years have seen a decline in church
attendance, and fewer people are following their religious
beliefs. Fewer men are entering the priesthood, despite the
fact that a Greek priest can almost be guaranteed a secure
income and social status within his community.

On the other hand, nearly every Greek person's life is
affected by religious rituals and feast days; Easter and the
Assumption of the Virgin (celebrated August 15) are the
most important events of the religious calendar. In contrast
to the commercial nature of Christmas in many countries,
Easter still has enormous spiritual significance to the Greeks.
It is a time when Greek people return to their home village

▲ *A modern Orthodox church
built in the Byzantine style*

IN THEIR OWN WORDS

I'm Mákis Giannakópoulos. I'm 14 years old and I was born here in
Athens. I go to church once or twice a month, usually because my
friends or grandparents ask me to go with them. During Easter
Holy Week I go every day. My family always goes to the Good
Friday evening service when we all follow the procession of the
Epitáfios that symbolizes Christ's funeral bier. Then on Saturday
night we celebrate Christ's resurrection. It's a great occasion.

Greece is becoming a less religious society. Young people and
teenagers like me have other idols to care about. We're interested
in pop stars and athletes. But Greek people are still superstitious.
Nearly everybody believes in *to máti*, or the evil eye, whatever
their background, wherever they live. Our families instill it in us as
children. The evil eye is connected to envy. If somebody admires
something about you, say a neighbor looks with admiration at a newborn child or something special
you've just bought, although they are intending you no harm, they may be casting the evil eye on
you. You may feel bad, perhaps feel sick or get a headache. Then you have to visit someone with
the power to take the evil away from you.

or town to join other family members in the local processions and rituals. Special Easter foods are cooked, and the Lenten fast, during which meat and other animal foods are not eaten, is still observed by many Greeks, including the young.

Foreign Influences

Name days have always been more important than birthdays in Greece. Each church, village, and town in Greece is associated with a particular saint, and most people are named after a saint. On their particular saint's day people are visited by friends and family who are offered a *kérasma*, or treat, of cakes and sweetmeats and, for the adults, sweet liqueurs. In recent decades, however, as a result of increased contact with other customs and traditions, more and more Greek children and young adults celebrate their birthdays, too.

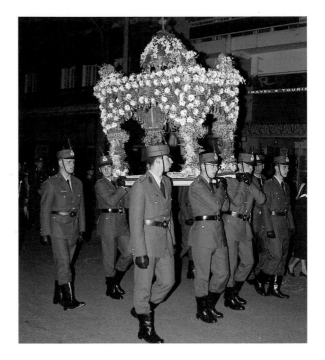

▲ *A recreation of Jesus' funeral bier is decorated with flowers for the Good Friday Epitáfios procession.*

▼ *At the end of the Easter Saturday mass, everybody carries home a lighted candle.*

Education

Greeks have always placed a high value on education. Children are encouraged to work hard beginning in their first school years. The state provides free education, from primary school through college. The school day is shorter than in many European countries but, alongside a large amount of homework, most children have after-school lessons in foreign languages or perhaps music. Many attend private schools in the afternoons and evenings for extra tutoring in their weaker subjects, especially if they are preparing for college entrance.

▲ *A group of children on their way home from school*

The education system has changed little in recent decades and the basic curriculum and teaching methods remain the same. The emphasis is still very much on learning facts rather than learning new ways of thinking.

As in many countries, Greek education is facing problems, such as low pay for teachers and a lack of facilities. Few schools have libraries, science laboratories, or computers. In urban schools, shortage of space is often a problem.

IN THEIR OWN WORDS

My name is Faní Balamóti. I am a teacher in a *lykeio*, or high school, for 15-to 18-year olds in Kalambáka, a town of 12,000 people. The school has about 100 students in each grade, which are divided into five groups. Altogether the students have an average of 35 school hours a week followed by three to four hours at a *frontistírio*, a private school, every day. There are also at least three hours of homework.

Most Greek families dream of a university degree for their children. When students fail to get into a Greek university they may go abroad to finish their education. I think students and their families should realize that a university degree is no longer a guarantee for employment and that they should be more open and flexible about their plans.

Sports and Leisure

Socializing with friends and family is the main leisure activity in Greece. This mainly takes place outside the home, in cafés and restaurants, especially during the summer when small city apartments become unbearably hot. Music is important to all generations of Greeks and is central to Greek culture. Much traditional Greek music, which combines Eastern and Western influences, is still played live at religious and cultural gatherings, as well as in taverns and clubs. During the summer months, lots of Greeks enjoy open-air concerts, plays, dance productions, and films.

▲ *Frappé, coffee blended with ice and served with milk or black, is a popular drink for young Athenians.*

The most popular sports are soccer and basketball, which are followed with passion. Sports are done mainly by the younger generations. Jogging, volleyball, swimming, sailing, and wind-surfing are the most popular sports.

► *City dwellers enjoy a weekend bike ride, unfortunately, bike helmets are rare in Greece.*

Diet and Health

For thousands of years Greek cuisine has changed very little. The traditional diet consists of plenty of vegetables, salads, and grains. Meat and fish are eaten about twice a week. Bread is eaten at every meal. However, recent decades have seen new trends in people's eating habits. The main meal of the day used to be prepared and cooked in the morning and eaten at a late lunch. As Greek wives and mothers are now going out to work, they are no longer able to shop on a daily basis and have little time to prepare a large midday meal. Consequently, there has been a trend not only toward eating the main meal in the evening, but also toward eating convenience and take-out foods.

Traditional Greek take-out foods are *souvlákia*, or kebabs, and cheese pies, but pizza and hamburgers are now found everywhere. Supermarkets have introduced people to many other "non-Greek" foods. In the past children seldom ate breakfast other than a glass of warm milk, but now many homes keep cereal in their cupboards.

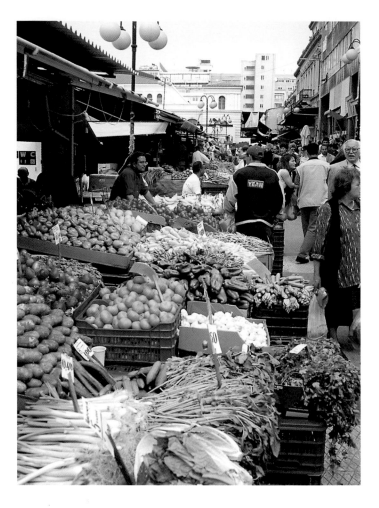

▲ *The majority of Greeks buy their fresh fruit and vegetables from street markets and greengrocers.*

◄ *American-style fast-food restaurants are common throughout Greece.*

IN THEIR OWN WORDS

My name is Yiannis Koutendakis. I like cooking "adventurous" food—like Spanish, Chinese, and Indian dishes. Of course that's not typical of Greeks. Greek men today still don't do a lot of cooking apart from barbecues and light meals, like pasta.

When I was growing up, our diet varied from season to season. Now we can buy whatever we want all through the year. We avoid fast food, except for an occasional pizza. You see lots of children snacking on potato chips and things. We give our children fruit rather than chips, though we do allow them chocolate, but almost never soft drinks. My family on Crete always supplies us with olive oil. In fact I never remember buying olive oil. Most people have a contact with an oil producer so they buy direct from them. In that way, things aren't so different from the past.

Health Provision

Greece's National Health System was established in 1983 to provide state-funded care. People are entitled to free treatment from doctors and pay only a small portion of their medicine costs. Today there are doctors in most villages.

The traditional Mediterranean diet, based on fresh produce, olive oil rather than animal fats, and little meat, is regarded as one of the healthiest in the world. However, as Greeks have become wealthier, they have increased their consumption of meat and processed foods. This change has brought new health problems such as obesity, heart disease, and diabetes.

▼ *Despite public awareness of the health risks associated with cigarettes, Greeks are some of Europe's heaviest smokers.*

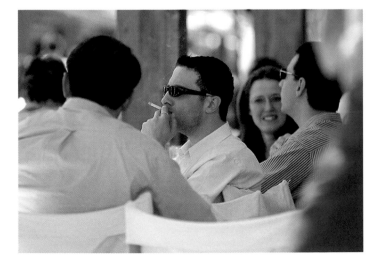

8

Changes at Work

Employment

Greece has traditionally been a country of small, family-run businesses. To be self-employed is usually seen as preferable to working for other people. With the exception of certain professions and the civil service, being an employee was seen as meaning you had little control over your working life, vacations, sick leave, or retirement fund. It also meant low wages. However, with rising industrialization and the emergence of large companies, employment conditions and job security prospects have improved. Today, of Greece's approximate 4.5 million employed people, 60 percent work in the service sector, and about 20 percent each in industry and agriculture.

▼ *Small shops, such as this specialist cured meat shop, are often family businesses with no or few paid staff.*

Women at Work

In the 1980s and 1990s, huge numbers of Greek women joined the salaried workforce. Today women make up over half the numbers employed in retailing and office jobs. Work in education, healthcare, and other areas of the civil service are considered particularly appropriate for women. Women also make up over 50 percent of the unskilled work force.

◀ *Athenian women shop in a pedestrian precinct. Athens has many chic and fashionable shopping districts.*

Source: International Labor Organization

Despite the existence of laws regarding equality of the sexes, women are still less likely to be in positions of management and responsibility. Women's salaries are often lower than those of their male colleagues, and when it comes to family businesses, they may not have an equal say in decision making.

▲ *The number of women in the workplace continues to grow as younger generations pursue careers rather than a traditional domestic role.*

IN THEIR OWN WORDS

My name is Ada Christophe. I run an English-language school. A lot of women in Greece are now doing jobs that were traditionally male jobs. You often see women driving buses and taxis. Women are forced to work now because life is so expensive. Few companies provide nurseries, so there is a growing demand for childcare. The state provides some preschool care, and it's free, but there is a need for much more. My working hours are between 4:00 P.M. and 10:00 P.M., which doesn't make it easy for me, since I am a single mother with a six-year-old son.

Manufacturing

Compared to other EU countries, Greece's industrial activity remains low. Long-established manufacturing industries include petrochemicals, cement, cigarettes, and textiles, including cotton goods and blankets. Greece no longer relies on imported domestic electrical appliances, since today it manufactures its own refrigerators, washing machines, and other electrical goods. In recent years food processing has become a particularly successful growth industry, while tourism has massively boosted the market for soft-drink industries. Most of the country's large industries are concentrated around Athens. Tourism has helped to sustain and generate new light-manufacturing industries (for example, pottery, woodwork, and souvenir making) in areas other than the big cities.

Evolving Industries

The last decade has seen the rapid rise of ownership of computers and mobile phones in all areas of Greek life. Today information technology, electronic commerce, and telecommunications are among

▲ The spread of tourism has brought about a huge increase in the number of people working in restaurants, bars, and cafés.

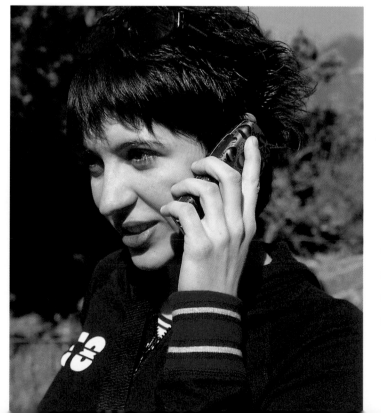

◄ Mobile phones are cheap to buy and use. Most Greek households now have at least one mobile phone.

IN THEIR OWN WORDS

My name is Theódoros Papatheódorou. I'm 23 years old and I work as a computer programmer for a bank. I write software to assess people's credit risk. In my free time I like to take photographs with my digital camera.

Most people have computers now. The Internet is the main reason that Greeks use them. Lots of young people have e-mail accounts, and nearly everyone has a mobile phone. Myself, I don't like mobile phones—I think they are a plague to the country. But I think mobile phone technology and the possibility of selling and buying online are the big things of the future. Most businesses have a website and online selling is growing. Greece is trying to become a center for information technology, rather like Ireland.

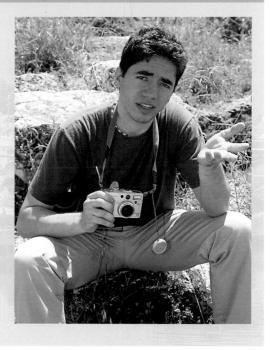

the fastest growing areas in the Greek economy, and many young Greeks are choosing to train and work in these fields.

Another evolving industry is wine making. Greeks have been making wine for thousands of years, but until very recently the wine industry was dominated by a handful of large companies. Today small wine businesses producing quality wines are found in Macedonia, the Peloponnese, and on some of the islands.

One of Greece's recent success stories is fish farms. These range from small businesses to large companies with several hundred employees. Helped by subsidies from the EU, the number and size of Greek fisheries has grown rapidly. With increasing exports of farmed sea bream and sea bass to Europe, fish farming is making an increasingly significant contribution to the country's economy.

▼ *Greece's coastline, with its countless bays, is ideally suited to fish farming.*

Shipping

With the largest merchant fleet in the world, shipping is a major contributor to Greece's economy. Other than Piraeus, Greece's biggest ports are Thessaloníki, Patrás, Vólos, and Heráklion. Until the end of the 1980s shipping was one of the largest employers within the private sector. In 1999 and 2000 there was a fall in the number of Greek shipping companies, partly because of increasing pressure on them to modernize and upgrade their vessels to meet international safety standards. However, the shipping sector is still expanding and Greek-owned ships still operate all over the world, although today their crews consist mainly of workers from other countries.

▲ *Piraeus is Greece's biggest port and one of the largest in the Mediterranean.*

Changing Patterns of Work

The working day in Greece varies according to the kind of business. For many Greeks, it may begin at 8:00 A.M. or

IN THEIR OWN WORDS

My name is Kóstas Epaminóndas. I'm from Limassol, on Cyprus, but now I live in Athens. I started a business selling cars here in 1993. Originally I sold BMWs, but now I specialize in Renaults. European cars sell well in Greece. There is no car manufacturing industry in the country and no cars are assembled here. All new cars have to be imported. About 250,000 new cars are bought every year. Despite the import duty, cars are cheaper in Greece than in many European countries. Gasoline is cheap, too. Most Greek families own at least one car. About ten years ago the government brought in tax concessions for people who traded in an old car for a new car. New cars are less harmful to the environment, and Athens has terrible pollution problems.

earlier, and end between 1:30 P.M. or 3:00 P.M. For others, (for example, those in retail), the working day may fall into two halves, with a long break for the afternoon siesta hours. In the cities this results in four, rather than two, rush hours, which contributes to pollution and congestion problems.

In the past the farming year dictated times of work and rest. For many Greeks now, it is the tourist season that determines this. In tourist areas, people regularly work for 17 or more hours a day, seven days a week, during the tourist season, as their shops, cafés, or offices stay open all day and late into the night. They then close their businesses between late October and the following spring. During these months, many people resume life in Athens or return to their villages either to tend to their land and crops or simply to recover from the long and hectic summer months.

Agricultural workers
(% of total working population)

54.0 — 1960
42.0 — 1970
31.0 — 1980
23.0 — 1990
20.0 — 1995

Source: Geographical Digest

▲ This graph shows Greece's strong reliance on agriculture in the past. This figure has decreased by more than half over the last thirty years.

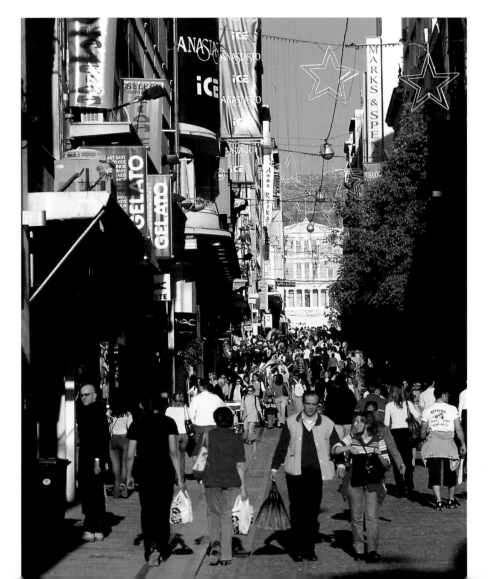

◄ In the summer, stores in Athens remain open late.

9

The Way Ahead

Greece lies at the crossroads between the East and the West. As a member of the EU, Greece is linked politically and economically with other member EU countries. Yet geographically, Greece is much closer to the other countries of southeast Europe. Political and economic events in the Balkans have had, and may continue to have, an enormous impact on Greece. During the 1990s, war and political turmoil in the former Yugoslavia and Albania meant that the main land route into Greece from Europe was cut off for many years. Political unrest also brought about mass immigration from that area. On the other hand, the collapse of Communism in southeastern Europe has led to the strengthening of Greece's trade links with its Balkan neighbors, including Turkey, although the two countries continue to have an uneasy relationship as a

▲ *The view from the Acropolis across Athens to Mount Lycabettus, the highest of the city's hills. The Greek national flag flies in the foreground.*

IN THEIR OWN WORDS

My name is Vangelis Thanos. My parents moved from the country to Athens, which they thought of as "the promised land," hoping to find a good job and an easier and more comfortable life. I am a percussionist with an orchestra. Europe has a great influence on the Greek people. We try hard to be like other Europeans, but we are beginning to lose our sense of community. And people don't care enough about things like pollution and the environment. They are more concerned with the present. I try to have a longer term attitude to life. The government and the media must make the environment a priority. There's too much political corruption in Greece. This has to change if we are to succeed as a country in the future. We have to change now if Greece in the future is to play a part in Europe and the world.

result of historical issues and the unresolved problem of Turkish-occupied Cyprus.

In the last 50 years Greece has transformed from a traditional, nonindustrial, agricultural society into a modern, prosperous, consumer-orientated society. At the turn of the 21st century, the rate of economic growth was faster than the average rate of that in other countries of the EU. Living standards have risen rapidly to a level above that enjoyed elsewhere in the Balkans. Great technological changes have taken place in a very short time. There have been vast improvements to the country's infrastructure, especially to that of Athens as it prepares for the 2004 Olympic Games. The problems confronting Greece today are similar to those faced by countries elsewhere, such as crises in education and health, environmental issues, rising unemployment, and immigration. Although there is a drug problem in the larger cities, overall there is relatively little poverty and crime, and family and community support is still strong. In Greece there is considerable optimism about the future, especially among the young.

▼ *The youth of Greece today has prospects that their grandparents could never have anticipated.*

Glossary

acid rain rain produced when sulphur dioxide and nitrogen oxides (gases released when fuels are burned) dissolve into rainwater to fall as sulphuric or nitric acid.

agriculture farming the land to produce food.

archipelago groups of many islands.

bier stand on which a coffin is placed and carried.

birth rate number of people born in a given area over a period of time.

cistern tank for storing water.

communists followers of Communism who believe that all people are equal and that all property should be publicly, as opposed to privately, owned.

consumer society society that is based on the purchase and consumption of goods and services.

culture beliefs, customs, language, and behavior shared by a group of people.

democracy system of government in which the population votes for the person or party who will govern them.

diaspora spread or dispersal of a people throughout the world.

economy all the business activity in a country.

emmigration leaving a country to live elsewhere.

European Union association of European countries that have joined together to cooperate on matters relating to trade, taxation, agriculture, the environment, etc.

fertilizers chemicals and other substances used to add nutrients to the soil.

hydroelectricity electricity that is generated by the use of running or falling water to turn turbines.

immigration coming to live in a country from abroad.

import to buy goods from other countries.

income money that people receive for their work or from their investments.

manufacturing making of goods.

mountain scrub brushwood and wild, shrub-like vegetation that grows wild on a mountain.

NATO North Atlantic Treaty Organization, an alliance of countries for the purposes of trade and security.

nomadic wandering way of life, often determined by the seasons and location of pasture land for animals.

peninsula piece of land that juts out into the sea.

pesticides chemicals used to destroy garden and crop pests.

population total number of people in a place at a given time.

raptors birds of prey.

rural relating to the countryside or nonurban areas.

subsidies government money that is given to a particular group to help with a specific project.

subsistence farming farming to produce food to support the farmer and his family as opposed to farming to produce crops for sale.

urban urban area that is built-up, such as a town or a city.

Further Information

Books to Read

Costain, Meredith. *Welcome to Greece.* Broomall, PA: Chelsea House, 2001.

Dubois, Jill. *Greece.* Tarrytown, NY: Marshall Cavendish, 2003.

Steele, Christy. *Greece (Ancient Civilizations).* Chicago: Raintree Publishers, 2001.

Useful Addresses

Greek National Tourism Office
168 North Michigan Avenue
Chicago, IL 60601
(312) 782-1084
www.gnto.gr/

Embassy of Greece
2221 Massachusetts Avenue
Washington, D.C. 20008
(202) 939-5800
www.greekembassy.org

United States Embassy in Athens
91 Vassilisis Sophias Avenue
Athens 10160
Greece
30-10-721-2951
www.usembassy.gr/

Index

Numbers in **bold** indicate pages where there is a photograph or illustration.

DATE DUE